WRITING FROM A GREEK ISLAND

ROGER SAWTELL

Copyright © 2019 Roger Sawtell

Published by PPR Publishing,
19 Kingswell Road, Northampton NN2 6QB.

www.pprpublishing.co.uk

All rights reserved

A CIP catalogue record for this book
is available from the British Library

ISBN: 978-1-9164347-4-5

Cover picture by Anna Mason

Drawings by Jayne Ruffell-Ward

Design by Nick Hamlyn

Roger Sawtell can be contacted at roger.sawtell@cooptel.net

Printed and bound in Great Britain by IngramSpark /
Lightning Source UK Ltd.

Writing From A Greek Island

Writing From A Greek Island

CONTENTS

Preface		3
1.	Sharing Bread	7
2.	Night on a Bare Mountain	12
3.	Brief Encounter	16
4.	"And Who is my Neighbour?"	17
5.	The Woman at the Well	19
6.	A Greek Tragedy Averted	21
7.	Second Coming	23
8.	The Boys on the Beach	25
9.	The Virgin and the Dagger	31
10.	Letter from a Barbary Pirate	36
11.	What to do About the Devil	38
12.	A Guide for Swimmers	40

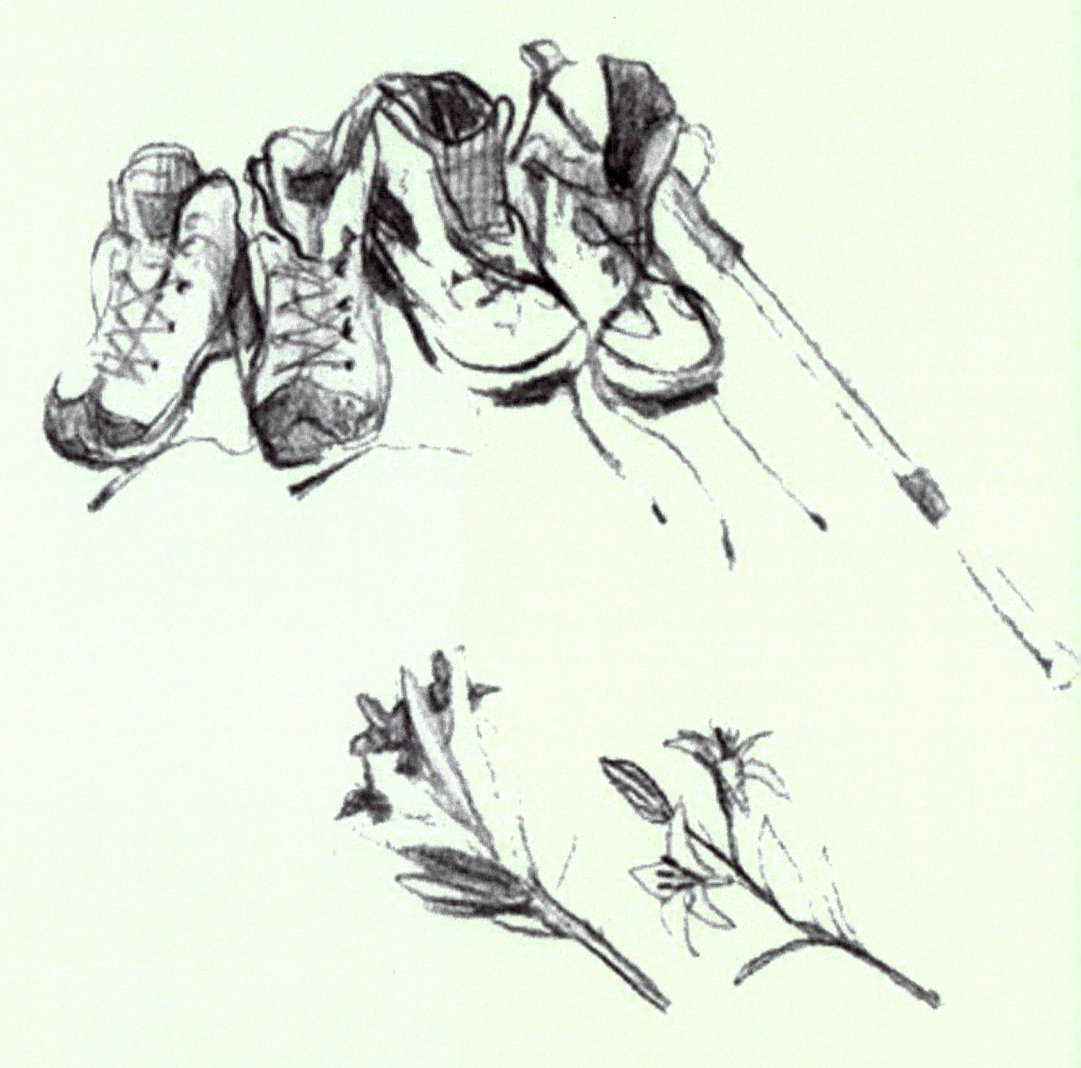

Preface

The common thread of these pieces, reflections, stories, swimming information, and even a poem, is that they are all connected with the island of *Amorgos*, the furthest east of the Cyclades. The stories are fiction rather than true in every detail, but like all fiction, they are a combination of the writer's experience together with imagination, and they are based on incidents that have happened to Susan and me as we have visited the island every year since 1993. Such experiences are received like potter's clay and moulded to the potter's liking, perhaps smoothing the rough edges and polishing the surfaces. Almost all the characters are entirely fictional but in a few incidents where necessary, I have changed the names to protect identity.

My grateful thanks are due to Jayne Ruffell-Ward for the drawings and to my granddaughter, Anna Mason, for the cover picture of *Theologos*. Thanks also to Margaret Williams in the UK and Marianna Lemonis on *Amorgos* for reading the text and making suggestions and corrections; and to Nick Hamlyn for turning the manuscript into a printed book.

Traditionally, the islanders were mainly dependent on fishing, farming, goats and sheep, and there were far more donkeys than cars in 1993. The road linking the east and west of the island was not yet tarmac and vehicles could be spotted miles away by the cloud of dust surrounding them. The ferry service was somewhat uncertain and tour companies avoided the island.

All this has changed during the last 25 years. The growing popularity of the Greek islands as tourist destinations and the advent of a large and reasonably reliable ferry have hugely increased the number of visitors and many of the islanders can make a living from providing rooms, tavernas, and cars for rent.

Every year the one road seems to get busier. The local baker trained in Lancashire and his patisserie would not look out of place on Kensington High Street. The darkened bars are patronised by heavyweight owners of visiting yachts including a few 'floating gin palaces', which may have gold-plated bathrooms.

However, away from the big beach at *Egiali* the charm of the island remains. The back country is unchanged, the small beaches remote and seldom visited, the hills beautiful and challenging for walkers. We have explored almost every track on the island, including the ridge walk which is listed in walking guides as one of the *'Twelve worldwide walks you must do before you die'*.

I am over ninety now and not quite as nimble as I would like to be, but my friend *Kostas* says, "Of course you will come back next year. I have a bottle of wine waiting for you." We shall see. Our annual visits have been life-enhancing and the people of *Amorgos* have given us much hospitality and shown us wisdom as we have walked on their hills, prayed in their churches, eaten in their tavernas. We are grateful.

Roger Sawtell   Northampton UK   June 2019

1. Sharing Bread – a reflection

There is an island in the Aegean sea, a line of hills against an azure sky. Until recently it was quite remote, not full of tourists, and there was not much night life compared with *Ios*, nor is there much rich agricultural land like *Naxos,* where the new potatoes grow. But there are beautiful beaches and hills to roam and friendly people.

The daily ferry to *Amorgos* in the 1990s was a funny old boat which rolled like a dog, pitched like a see-saw, and combined the two into a hideous corkscrew motion guaranteed to make most of the passengers sick. Paper bags were provided free. The crew collected the fares in an old Nescafe tin and there was an aspidistra in a large pot in the wheelhouse. We never knew until the last minute if the *Skopo* – for that was the name of this rustbucket – would set sail, because *Amorgos* is at the far side of a notorious patch of rough water, famous for its heavy swell. However we learned that the captain and crew lived on the island and liked to get home every night, so she usually rolled and pitched her way across the wine-dark sea, sometimes arriving after midnight. Little wonder that in those days there were few visitors and the island was eschewed by tour companies who need reliable schedules to ensure their clients get home on time. On one occasion we were stranded on a neighbouring island, *Donoussa,* for three days, waiting for the weather to abate and the *Skopo* to arrive. Bread was running low.

For hundreds of years wheat was grown on the terraces behind the village here, brought down to the beautiful circular stone threshing-floors that still abound on the island. In 1993 we saw five donkeys trudging slowly round a threshing circle near *Kolofana.* The donkeys had nose-bags to limit them from eating too much. The women were then forking-up the wheat high in the air to separate the grain from the chaff. Too much wind would blow away the grains and too little would not blow away the chaff, so the weather had to be just right for this vital winnowing process.

Historically the donkeys would then have taken the grain up to the high mountain ridge which is the spine of the island, where there are the remains of four massive windmills which ground the flour for three villages. The windmills stopped grinding in the 20th century and sheep now use the crumbling towers for shelter. The wrought iron nails which held the mechanism together can be used to make pendant neck crosses.

The older people who have lived here all their lives remember some of these fundamental processes and so it is not surprising that bread is regarded as a necessity with every meal, even though most of the flour now comes in by ferry. The significance of bread is also apparent when the waiter in a taverna on *Amorgos* comes to take your order. He brings the knives and forks and also a basket of bread. How can you eat a Greek meal without a thick slice of bread? This is the default position and if you do not want bread you have to say so.

When the remote monastery of *Theologos* was being restored in the 1990s, one of the tasks was to rebuild the bread oven, fired with aromatic bushes gathered on the hillside. We have had the privilege of taking part in preparing the dough, pushing eggs into it in their shells, and then baking it in the dying embers. At *Theologos,* such bread, eaten fresh with local fish and washed down with the dark *mavro* local wine, makes an unforgettable meal.

This island is mountainous and beautiful, but does not have much agricultural land. There used to be trees, but a great fire destroyed most of them in 1835 and those that remain are ravaged by goats which run free over the mountains and eat any green shoot unwise enough to show itself. So now, apart from olive orchards, there are few trees and we know most of them as friends, where we can find shade and eat our picnic away from the midday sun.

The goats appear to be feral but in fact many have bells and now and again they are rounded up by wily shepherds for goat stew. The old *Skopo* used to carry smelly bundles of goatskins to some tannery. Once we met a man who wore a goats hair vest. I don't think he took it off between December and March. He was out in the hills shearing his goats in a shelter, perhaps to enable his loyal wife to knit him a spare vest.

One day in 1993 we were walking on the ridge, far from any habitation, and met a shepherd with a flock of the rather raggedy sheep which roam the hills. He had a dark straggly beard and seemed an integral part of the landscape, along with thorn bushes and outcropping rocks, all a similar mixture of brown and grey. Although he was carrying nothing but a leather shoulder bag, we got the impression that he had been living out on the hills for some days with his flock. He was having his lunch and invited us by gesture to sit and join him. Without any ceremony he produced pieces of hard dry bread from the bottom of his bag and handed it to us as we might offer a fresh cucumber sandwich at a tea party. It seemed his natural response to anyone he might meet in his solitary life and he did not expect any thanks or acknowledgement but assumed we would eat his dry crusts with him. We were embarrassed to offer in return our picnic lunch including apples and digestive biscuits but he showed little interest in such trivialities and considered it a great joke. We had almost no words in common but I think he might have said, "What do you want all that fancy stuff for, when all you need is this good bread baked by my wife down in the village last week?" We thanked him and I wondered why we needed to carry so much equipment, rucksacks, sandwich boxes, and even a knife with a special spike for removing stones from horses' hooves. I never seemed to come across a horse requiring a stone to be removed and the donkeys were too experienced to get stones in their hooves, so I decided to dispense with it.

On another occasion, walking in the hills far from any habitation, we were passing a small church and were surprised to see a group of people standing outside it. There are nearly a hundred churches on *Amorgos,* as every land-owning family has its own church, many of them in remote places. Some are locked but many are open, sometimes with an oil-light burning, indicating that a family member is visiting regularly. Each church has an annual festival when there is a service followed by a meal. On this occasion there had been a service and they were coming out of the church, including the Papas in his stove-pipe hat, all talking at the same time, as they do in Greece. Each was holding a piece of the blessed bread from the eucharist and as we passed, total strangers in a foreign land, they smiled and broke-off a piece of bread for us to eat. We learned that this was the custom of the Orthodox church, to share the remaining bread with strangers and we ate it with thanksgiving.

Over the years we have visited about fifty of these country churches, lighting a candle, resting in their shade, sometimes burning fragrant incense, saying a prayer. At the larger churches in the villages and those attached to the monastery, the festivals are important social events to which local people come in their best clothes, some on foot and some by donkey. The service can last several hours and the custom is for the congregation to come and go, but nearly all stay for the traditional *patatato,* a substantial meal of goat stew and potato cooked in a large iron cauldron. Visitors are welcomed, bread and wine are shared.

The symbolism of this simple sharing of bread is surely significant. There is enough bread to feed the whole world, but only if we share it. At the time of writing there is famine in South Sudan and in Yemen and yet the news is that a picture by Leonardo da Vinci was auctioned recently in New York for $450 million. If we are unwilling or incapable of sharing, we destroy not only the poor but, in due course, we destroy ourselves.

Back in the UK, Jake, standing outside a pub, says, "Got any dough, mate?" He is not referring to making bread but merely using one of the multitude of slang words for money, along with dosh, bread and honey, lolly, moolah. Bread in one form or another is a basic necessity.

2. Night on a Bare Mountain – a reflection

To Yahweh belongs the earth... and all who live there;
it is he who laid its foundations on the seas...
Who shall go up to the mountain of Yahweh ?
Who shall take a stand in his holy place ?

Psalm 24 'For a solemn entry into the sanctuary'

This was a rare experience. It is unusual for any of us, with or without a companion, to spend a night in the knowledge that there is no other person, asleep or awake, within three kilometres.

The uninhabited early-Byzantine monastery of *Theologos* (Word of God) stands 400 metres above the sea on a remote headland on the coast of *Amorgos*. It fell into disrepair in the 20th century; goats got in and rubble accumulated in the aisles but fortunately the roof was secure. Then for twenty years starting in the 1990s, it was slowly and lovingly restored, mostly by two local retired stone masons, assisted by summer working parties of volunteers.

It is indeed a sanctuary, a quiet place of safety. The rugged building blends seamlessly into the hillside so that it is difficult to distinguish the rock which is millions of years old from the man-made structure which is a mere one thousand years old. There are huge buttresses to withstand the weather on this exposed site and all is whitewashed, both rock and building. Part of the seating in the church is rough living rock, not smoothed by the builders but deliberately left as a symbol that man is dependent on Yahweh, *'who laid its foundations'*.

There are no monks living at *Theologos*. We are told that a local monk hopes to live there one day so that it would again become a working monastery. The bread oven has been rebuilt, the well is full and there is even a 'squat loo', down which one may pour buckets of water.

It is an hour's uphill walk from the nearest village, hundreds of paved steps, which have been polished by donkeys' hooves for a thousand years. There is a profound silence in this hill country, a silence not found on the plains and never in the city. It is more positive than absence of noise, so that the occasional mournful bleat of a goat or the cry of an unknown bird do not seem to break the silence but rather to add to it as an integral part of a landscape that has hardly changed since the early Cycladic people came to live here. It is a pervasive natural silence which differs from our domestic attempts to create quietness by shutting the kitchen door to keep out the hum of the fridge or drawing the curtains to eliminate the traffic noise. Subconsciously we know that these noises continue out of earshot whereas at *Theologos* there is no such extraneous noise.

One summer in the cool of the evening, we walked up, just the two of us, made supper as darkness fell, and lit candles in the church for evening prayers. In God's presence, we remembered friends who have visited this place with us in previous years. It was a clear evening and where there are no houses or street lights, the stars are sharper.

We slept well in the monastery dormitory and were up at daybreak to watch the sun come up from the sea and shine straight through the east window, lighting up the altar and the *iconostasis.* No need for huge east windows like the northern European cathedrals, just two narrow slits in the massive east wall of this church are enough for the heavens to declare the glory of God in this place. And perhaps those early builders, men of deep faith to build in such a remote place, knew that there is no land between *Theologos* and Jerusalem so that, if they had been able to see over the horizon, a thousand kilometres to the east, they would see this same sun reflecting upon the golden dome of the Temple Mount and the streets where Jesus walked.

Hill walkers visit *Theologos* because it is in the guidebooks, but some never see the rugged interior of the church because the huge key to the west door must be turned twice clockwise whereas most of us are conditioned to unlock doors anti-clockwise, one turn. Maybe some mischievous monk deliberately installed the lock upside down as a symbol that Christianity can be considered an upside-down religion? The poor are to be given preference over the rich and it was the hated but humble tax collector, not the Pharisee, who went home '*at rights with God*' (Luke 18:14).

Janey O'Shea (Backhouse Lecture 1993 *Living the Way*) writes:-

> **'In the topsy-turvy world of the way of God as taught by Jesus, familiar categories turn upside down; people with contagious diseases are touched and healed; a woman**

who prefers intellectual discussion to housework is highly valued; the unemployed get a day's wage for a few hours work; a prostitute is held up as a good example to a religious leader; the good seats at a state banquet go to the street people…'

With these upside-down concepts ringing in our ears, we gave thanks for the opportunity to be in this special place and walked back down the hill to what we call normal life.

3. Brief Encounter

I met a man among the far-distant hills,
remote, blessed with no signal,
the rock fissiparous, the stones too hot to touch,
parched as we were parched, needing to tell our stories.

He spoke of friends, of love found and lost,
of faith lost but found again by gift.
He spoke of Jesus, roaming the hills of Galilee.
I too told my story.

He knows not my name, nor I his.
I doubt we shall ever meet again,
but there was value in our meeting,
fleeting, existential. I shall not forget.

4. "And Who is my Neighbour ?" (Luke 10:29)

Megali Vlichadha is a remote sandy bay on the northeast coast of Amorgos. It is enclosed by steep slopes and cliffs, so there is no path and only a risky scramble down the cliff-face. It is seldom visited. After several failed attempts, Susan and I have twice reached this bay (and returned safely!) On the way down we tied ribbons to bushes to enable us to find the way back. The story that follows is loosely based on an actual incident which occurred in 2003.

On a remote and mountainous island in the Aegean sea there is a small sandy bay protected by a steep cliff. Walkers look down from the clifftop 150 metres above this bay and most turn back when they see the precipitous route down the cliff-face.

Francois is an experienced walker in the French Alps near his home. The day is hot and the bay below looks delectable. He decides not to be deterred by the steepness of the cliff and notices that there are some small cairns of stones marking the route. He scrambles carefully down the cliff, jumping the last two metres on to the sand. The water is crystal clear and he has a swim and a picnic. He uses his mobile phone to tell his friends in France about his adventure. "Wish we were there with you," they say, "here it is raining."

Francois examines the bottom of the cliff but cannot see quite where to start the way back. The first few metres look inaccessible from below so he explores the area behind the beach where there is a dried-up stream bed. But this soon leads to a narrow gorge and a vertical fall. There is no way he can ascend it and there is no other apparent way to get out. Returning to the beach and realizing that it is getting late, he decides to attempt to climb the rockface but cannot find a hold, misses his footing and falls back onto the beach, landing heavily. He has damaged his ankle which soon swells up and is very painful. He can hardly hobble, let alone climb, so he uses his phone to contact the police.

"We are busy," says the policeman, "and I cannot leave my post. We cannot help you, but here is the number of an English person who lives on the island and knows the paths."

"Yes," says Donald, "I can come and show you the way out. I will charge you 100 euro."

"To hell with that," says Francois, who is tough. "I would rather die here of starvation than pay you 100 euro."

So he phones the police again. "We cannot help you. We are very busy and you are stupid to go to that bay. Here is the number of a local person who owns a taverna in the village a few kilometres from the bay."

"Yes," says Yannis at the taverna, "I will come straight away and help you." So he saddles his donkey, Plato, takes him along the path, tethers him at the top of the cliff, and quickly descends to the beach, as he has done many times before. Guided and supported step by step by Yannis, Francois is just able to make the ascent. but with considerable difficulty due to his injured leg. At the top Yannis puts the exhausted Francois on to Plato, who seems to understand that he is carrying an injured person and steps delicately and sure-footedly over the rough ground, back to the taverna in the village. Yannis gives him a meal and then takes him in his battered pick-up truck to the doctor at the other end of the island, who says Francois has a serious sprain and must rest-up for several days if he wants to avoid a permanent disability.

"I am booked to start my journey home to-morrow," says Francois, "and I have no more money."
"No problem," says Yannis, "My friend Nikos has rooms here where you can stay. You can pay me back if you come again next year."

"Nikos, please will you look after this young man. He needs a room for a few days to get his ankle better. Please pay for whatever he needs and I will give you the money next time I am passing."

In the story of The Good Samaritan, Jesus asks, "*Which of these three was a neighbour to the man...?*"

5. The Woman at the Well
– a biblical reflection on John 4:11

> The woman said to Jesus, "Sir, it's a deep well and you haven't even got a bucket. How are you going to get the constant supply of water you're talking about?"
>
> 'Good As New – a radical re-telling of the Scriptures'
> John Henson (O Books 2004)

This island is dotted with wells, many of them in remote places no longer used for pasturing sheep or goats; they are evidence that much of the land was previously used for grazing animals made possible by the vital presence of water. Now there are more visitors than sheep and those who venture into the back country and explore the wonderful hills and valleys need water in this hot dry climate. We are approaching the remote ninth century uninhabited monastery of *Theologos* and I know there is a well of good water on the *platia* at the church, but no bucket and no habitation within several kilometres. This church is a favourite place for us; the walls and floor have been replaced over the centuries but one of the side benches is the solid living rock, not made by man. So one may sit here in the knowledge that monks will have sat on this same rock a thousand years ago, a similar experience to walking on the stony shore of Lake Galilee in the knowledge that one may well be treading on the same stones as Jesus did two thousand years ago.

We need water, but few walkers carry a bucket, so some ingenuity is required. With a sharp knife, cut the top off a one-litre bottled water container such as are sold in every shop and *cafenion*. With the knife point punch two holes, diametrically opposite each other, near the top of the beheaded bottle. Find a suitably-sized stone, the heavier the better, to fit into the bottom of the bottle as a sink weight. Now thread through the holes a neck cord or bootlaces tied together or similar and lower the bottle into the well to draw up refreshing water. We have used this Boy Scout procedure on numerous occasions. However, today there is a problem. For good reason, knives are banned by airlines and mine has been confiscated at the check-in, so I have no means of adapting a water bottle. But help is at hand.

Usually we have this special place to ourselves and have spent quiet days here, sitting in the church and picnicking on the *platia*. No monks have lived here for many years and there is no road to Theologos, only a donkey track, so the only visitors are hill-walkers who pass by. However, today, to our surprise and pleasure, we are greeted by Katerina. The authorities of the Orthodox Church have invited her to spend the summer months in residence in the frugally restored monastic rooms, to welcome passing walkers and offer the traditional *raki* and *loukoumi*. Her smiling presence augments this special place where prayers have been said for over a thousand years. I count it a blessing and an example of truly Christian hospitality to strangers, irrespective of faith or no faith or somewhere in between. "You have no bucket to draw water," says Katerina, "but I will fetch mine from the dormitory." So our water bottles are replenished and our spirits also. Though our conversation does not quite proceed in the manner of John 4:11, there is value in this meeting and I give thanks. *Kyrie Elaison*.

6. A Greek Tragedy Averted
– a dramatised version of a real-life event

A large turtle has arrived in the bay and is swimming about by the quay. This is unusual and we have never seen such a turtle here previously. They are known to breed on the southern shores of Turkey and the locals, gathered at the *cafenion* are agreed that it must have come from there, 100 kilometres across the unpredictable Aegean Sea. So it was considered to be a Turkish turtle, not a Greek resident, but it would be made welcome because Greeks know about the pain of having to leave one's homeland and, on this and other nearby islands, they have been generous and welcoming to the overwhelming numbers of refugees arriving on their shores, fleeing from the disastrous civil war in Syria during the last few years.

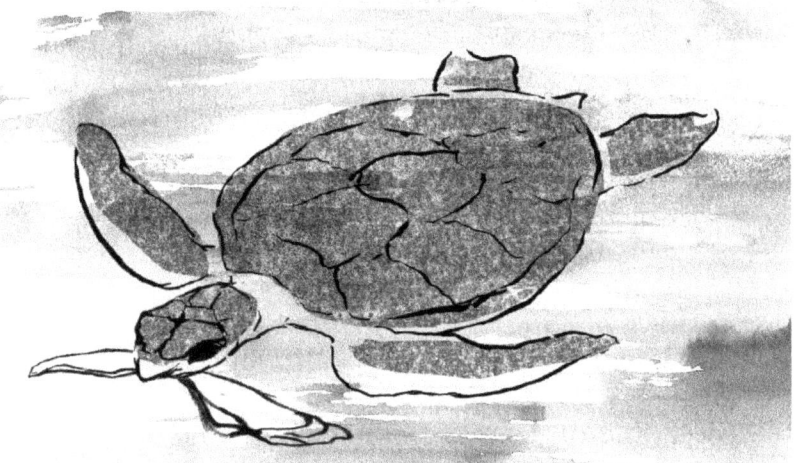

Then bad news reaches the *cafenion;* it seems the turtle has tried to eat a plastic bag in the water and is in danger of suffocating. *Dimitri*, a fisherman, has managed to lift it gently out of the sea and put it into a water storage tank on the quay, but help is needed if the turtle's life is to be saved. The nearest vet is on *Naxos*, fifty kilometres away. What to do? There is much heated discussion and loud shouting amongst those who know little about the ways of turtles. However, it is agreed by a majority vote that, due to its Turkish nationality it shall be called *Constantinople,* or *Conni* for short, not knowing how to detect the difference between a male

and a female turtle.
"Where is its thing?" says young *Adoni*, but no one can answer him.

The next important question for the assembly is how to transport a large sick turtle to *Naxos*. *Dimitri* wields an electric drill and shouts that he will drill a hole in the turtle's shell, pass a strong cord through it and tow *Conni* to *Naxos* behind his fishing boat.

"*Dimitri*, you are a stupid fool," yells *Yorgos*, "*Conni* would never survive such treatment." The argument then gets so heated that there is pushing and shoving among the younger men and the pocket of *Yanni's* jeans gets ripped. He shows the tear to his friend and shouts "*Euripides!*" – an old school joke. "Nonsense," says his friend, "I never ripped them. His long-suffering mother will repair them. Stuff a plastic bag down his throat to keep him quiet."

"Well," says old *Elias*, a plumber, "there are plenty of large old communal cooking pots at the village dump."
We fill one with water, put it on my pick-up truck, and take *Conni* on the Blue Star ferry, only two hours to *Naxos*."

"But the water will slop about on the car deck," says *Stavros*, who works on the ferries, "and anyway, what kind of ticket is available for a turtle of unknown gender? The Captain would not approve. No, we must smuggle *Conni* on board in a large plastic sack and then release him in the shower tray in the men's room on B deck."
"But what if *Conni* is female," says *Elias*, "she would not be allowed in the men's room. It would not be proper."

Further ribald comments are drowned out by the noise of a helicopter landing on the quay. The vet has arrived from *Naxos*. All is well. Everyone congratulates each other on their wisdom in solving the problem. More ouzo is called for.

7. Second Coming - *a Christmas story*

(Based on a true incident which occurred in 2010)

On a little-known Greek island, we are walking up a steep track to visit the remote monastery of Theologos, Word of God, which stands on a rugged plateau 300 metres above the sea. Built in the 9th century, it has recently been lovingly restored by local builders. There is no intervening land between Theologos and Jerusalem, a thousand kilometres to the east. If we had a sufficiently powerful telescope we might be able to see the sun reflecting on the golden dome of the Temple Mount and, perhaps, the road to Bethlehem, with a military checkpoint and the hideous separation wall barring the way, for Bethlehem is on the West Bank, under military occupation by the Israeli army, not unlike the Roman military occupation two thousand years ago .

We have been here many times but each time is different and today, as we are toiling up the path, we meet a party coming down . This is surprising because no one lives at Theologos and there is no habitation at this end of this wild island. The nearest village is several kilometres behind us and usually there would be no one on this path except for the occasional shepherd visiting his goats. A young man with a beard and a stout stick is leading a donkey on which a young woman is sitting. They are dressed in dark homespun clothes and, clearly, they are not visitors like us. Despite the summer sun, they look like a million Christmas cards. I say "Kalimera," one of my few Greek words. He smiles and replies, "To you, good morning."

I compliment him on his English pronunciation and he tells me he has worked on construction sites in western Europe. He is a carpenter. He was born in the south of this island where his parents still live and today they are travelling there to register for voting in the European election.

The girl is quiet and her face is half-hidden by a shawl. The man tells us that his fiancée has discovered she is pregnant and the baby may soon be born. "It is a great mystery for us because we sleep not in the same bed. It is not our custom here, but next year we shall be married, if it is God's will. I love her much and will protect her and the baby." The girl whispers something and he translates, "She says that God has told her that the baby will be a boy and will be a great blessing to many peoples. We believe it, both, and we must hurry down this path for we are told there is many visitors at the tavernas just now and maybe no rooms for us."

"Every blessing on you both," we say, "and on your son when he is born. We shall pray for you."
"Epharistho, thank you," he replies, and asks us our names, as many Greeks do.
"I am Roger and my wife is Susan."
He says, "My fiancée is Maria and I am Josef."
They travel on down the path.

The next day, back in the village where we are staying, no one else seemed to have seen them, but Theologos is a 'thin' place where there is not much space between God and humankind.

8. The Boys on the Beach

In the summer of 2015 hundreds of thousands of Syrians fled from the devastating civil war in their country. Many of these refugees went to Turkey and then attempted to cross the sea to nearby Greek islands to gain entry into the European Union. What follows is fiction, but based on actual events.

They wearily waded ashore from their collapsing inflatable, a motley group in dark clothes, mostly young men but also children and some mothers with babies. The older people had been unable to tackle the hazardous journey through Turkey. They had stayed behind in Aleppo, hoping the war would end but it had not ended and many of them would by now have died from the bombing.

On the beach, some knelt down on the golden sand to give thanks for reaching safety. But was it safe? Where were they? Would they be received with friendship or hostility? They were exhausted, had brought nothing with them, no spare clothes, nothing to shelter them from the sun and no blankets for the cold nights. They had left Turkey the day before, about fifty of them crammed into an inadequate boat, to make the short crossing to Kos, only five miles away. But the motor had failed halfway across. Maybe the fixer had not put enough petrol in the tank , so they had drifted past Kos, helplessly westward all night and most of the following day across what Homer had called the 'wine-dark sea'. One of the older men had died during the night and they had had no option but to cast his body into the sea, muttering a hurried prayer for the journey of his soul. Now they were blown on to this unknown beach and they stood together, a dark group on the sand like an inkblot on a clean page.

The holiday makers, mostly from western Europe, in their multi-coloured bikinis, sipping cold drinks, endlessly clutching their smartphones, gazed at them incredulously. One of the village elders, uncertain what to do about this unexpected arrival right on his doorstep, sent for his grandson, Dimitri, a scholarly boy of sixteen. He never tired of telling anyone who would listen that one day Dimitri would be prime minister of Greece. His grandfather said he had an old head on his young shoulders, but Dimitri said it was a good head for football which was more important than being prime minister.

During the years when Greece was awarded large amounts of European Union money, many of the young people on the island had moved to the bright lights of Athens and traditional agriculture had declined. However, some of the local people had built *domatia*, rooms to rent, and had become comfortably prosperous by attending to the the needs of the visitors who rented them. This is a small island and not a well-known tourist destination like Mykonos or Crete. Some of the older people spoke only a little English but the island had become the choice of discerning western visitors who enjoyed the hills and the huge curving beach like a horizontal crescent moon.
"Go away," said the village elder in Greek, "we don't want you here."

The Syrians gazed at him uncomprehendingly and did not move.
"Dimitri, tell them in English to go away."
"OK grandpa," said Dimitri, "but how can they go away? Their boat is kaput and they have nowhere to go."
"I can't help that. Just tell them. Our livelihood depends on visitors who will not come here if there are dozens of destitute people messing up the beach and pissing among our olive trees."
So Dimitri, who learned English at school, shouted, "We ask you to go away!"
There was silence, no one seemed to understand, no one moved. Then young Mohamed, who also had English from his school in Aleppo, a hub of the old trade routes from Europe to Asia, said, "How can we go? Where shall we go?"

Dimitri said, "Grandpa, this year in school we have been studying the history of our island. We were helpless refugees when the Venetians sacked the island in 1300 and, much later when we were invaded by pirates, our people fled to Turkey where they took us in and we stayed for 30 years until it was safe to return to our beloved island. When a Jesuit priest visited here in the 18th century he was impressed with the hospitality he received, despite the poverty of the island, and he declared, '*A stranger is a friend, sent by God, to whom dry bread and hard beds are offered with an open heart.*' Surely, let us continue our reputation for friendship. Let us embrace these unfortunate people from Syria and give them food and shelter."
One of the elders said, "They will shit on the beach and ruin our tourist trade. Dimitri, see what they say."

Then the Mayor arrived and a group of local people gathered round, muttering to each other. The boy's eloquence moved them to reconsider their hostility and their consciences were touched. The Mayor was concerned for the people of the island but he was not unsympathetic to the refugees; his own grandfather had lost his home when the Germans had occupied the island during World War II.

Among the Syrians, those with sufficient energy surrounded Mohammed to discuss, but many just lay down on the sand, too exhausted to take part. Then Mohammed approached Dimitri and they smiled at each other as any teen-aged boys might do, exchanged names and even shook hands in front of all the people.

"Oh Dimitri," said Mohammed, "we are helpless. If you cannot help us we will die here on this beautiful beach, alongside your visitors in their bright clothing, clutching their smartphones and covering themselves with suncream."

"Hi Mohamed," said Dimitri, "you are a Muslim and I am a Christian but we share the same creator God. It is strange that you and I are the only ones here who can understand one another. It is a heavy responsibility. The Mayor is an important man but I will entreat with him."

The Mayor remained uncertain but allowed himself to be persuaded. "I am the Mayor. I am elected to represent the people of our island. I will not be pushed about. Dimitri, tell them in your best English that we will provide water and food and shelter but first they must register, every one, at my office, with their name, age and occupation. We will then discuss what is to be done."

There is plenty of food on the island and the people were not ungenerous. They know their island story and they understood and responded to Dimitri's historical references. Soon they brought quantities of bottled water, set-up cooking fires on the beach and made *souvlaki* and *falafal*. Milk was brought for the babies as the mothers had little to give. It was decided to restore an old campsite behind the beach and, led by Dimitri's uncle who was a builder, a mixed working party of Greeks and Syrians spent several days building shelters, restoring the water supply to standpipes and digging new latrines.

But what about the tourists on the beach? Dietrich from Dusseldorf looked at the ragged mob with disgust. "I have worked hard and saved money all the year for my family to come here for a holiday and now it is spoilt by these dreadful people." But his wife disagreed. "Remember, Dietrich, your grandparents in Dusseldorf were bombed out of their house and lived in a cellar until the war ended in 1945. Then, remember, they told us some people from England came over and helped them to rebuild some houses. They were called Quackers or something, but they mostly kept silent and did not quack like ducks. Also, my grandparents fled from the eastern border to avoid the Russian advance at the end of the war. My parents had nothing, no toys and only the clothes they were wearing but they were made welcome, and look at us now. We have much to be thankful for."

Then Jens from Sweden, with two young children, chipped in, "In Sweden we have received many refugees from Syria. They are good workers. We must help these people by collecting money for them to buy food. We are rich and they have lost everything. Görrel, empty the sand out of your bucket and we will use it to collect money." So Jens and his daughters, with Mohammed and Dimitri, walked along the beach with the bucket. Some ignored them, one man scowled and threw sand at Jens but others dug in their pockets and gave a euro or a spare sweater and some put in notes of €10 and €20. One elderly German said he had been a refugee as a child, put in €50 and offered more. Jens gave the money to Mohammed and even the village elder seemed pleased, perhaps because he knew that some of it would be spent at his mini-market.

The Syrians duly registered at the mayor's office and it was found that many of them had skills which the Greeks needed because there were so few young people now living on the island. Some were builders and carpenters and dressmakers, two were motor mechanics and one was a doctor. They put their skills at the disposal of the islanders. There was mutual respect and friendships began to develop.

Dimitri and Mohammed formed rival football teams and many hard-fought matches were played on the beach. The Syrians called Dimitri 'Dim', which seemed rather inappropriate because he is anything but dim, but it was a sign of their respect for him as the vital go-between. In response, he called Mohammed 'Ma', which also seemed inappropriate for a teenage boy, but did acknowledge the motherly concern he was showing for his people in their traumatic situation.

After a few weeks the refugees had replaced the shelters on the campsite with simple breeze-block cabins to withstand the winter and also made some new benches for the village square where all the business was done. A skilled Syrian stonemason carried out some repairs to the local Orthodox church. There was only one part-time doctor on the island, doing her national service, so the Syrian doctor helped out at the surgery. A group of women worked out how to turn their orange lifejackets into colourful shoulder bags, with the plastic whistles still attached They sold them to visitors and gave the money to the mayor to help to pay for the food provided for them.

Nevertheless, many of them were saddened because of their plight and mourned those who had died during their long journey from Aleppo. Some of the islanders remained angry about the presence of the Syrians but most accepted them with continuing hospitality.

At the end of the summer Dimitri went back to school. His English Literature teacher told him to read John Donne's poems and quoted,

> *"No man is an island, entire in itself ………*
> *any man's death diminishes me because*
> *I am involved in mankind."*

9. The Virgin and the Dagger – a short story

On the remote southern coast of a Greek island there is a semi-derelict church, within what was once a walled enclosure of about an acre, with olive trees. It was thought to have been a small monastic community linked to Chozoviatissa. Now it is seldom visited. In the tiny church there is a faded fresco of Virgin Mary with a dagger in her bosom, painted during a restoration in about 1780.

This was also a time of pirate raids on Amorgos. The monks living there may not have been aware of the verse in Luke's Gospel, 'and a sword will pierce your own soul too' (Luke 2:35).

There are six of us living here at Hrisostomos, keeping the vigils, growing our own food, praying daily for our brothers and sisters in the world outside. It's a hard life and although our mother house, the big monastery, is only a mile or two away, the path is difficult, the cliffs are very steep and Father Abbot only visits us once or twice a year. However, we have olive trees and fruit in season and we grow wheat and barley in the walled compound which keeps the goats out. And, most important, we are blessed with a spring of good water and have built a well in the porch of our little church. Father Abbot, on his occasional visits, never fails to remind us that Jesus, one thousand seven hundred years ago, described his message of salvation as 'living water'. Brother Yanis, always a joker, says, "But Father, do you have a bucket?" No one else would dare to speak to Father Abbot in such a light-hearted manner.

In winter, gales may blow for days on end and there is only just enough firewood for baking our daily bread, let alone heating our living quarters. Last winter, Brother Giorgis caught a cold, had trouble with breathing and died within a week, despite our efforts to keep him warm with infusions of sage which grows all over our hillside. Mind you, the rest of the year is sunny on our plateau, facing south, and it is full of flowers and herbs for us to use. Father Abbot has travelled and he tells us that there is no intervening land between us and Jerusalem, many miles to the east, and if we had eyes good enough we would be able to see the morning sun reflected on the golden dome of the Temple. Just above our church there is a cave in the cliff face, where Brother Adonis has lived for the last three years, never once coming out. Needless to say, he is a contemplative and we accept that he can be nearer to God, living in this hermit's cell, than anywhere else. He has his own water supply from a rock which drips good water at the back of the cave and he has gouged out a channel and a hollow in the solid rock in which the water collects for him to drink. He asked us to build a wall across the front of the cell after he had entered and there is no door but just an open window looking out over the sea, with some other islands just visible on a clear day. A wonderful view. We take him bread and olives three times a week and put them on his window sill but he seldom answers when we call out a friendly greeting, "Brother, is there anything you need?" However, we hear him singing from time to time so we think he must be happy. I wonder how long he will stay there. We will certainly not try to dissuade him because there can be no higher purpose than being close to God who created the world.

We are committed to share with the poor, as Jesus did, but we get few visitors here and fewer still who are poorer than us! Some years ago a large ship anchored off our bay and the crew came ashore as it is one of the few places where landing is possible on the south coast of our island, which has massive cliffs for most of its length. They were a rough-looking mob, armed with long swords and knives so we realised they were pirates and most of us ran to hide in the caves for fear of getting our throats cut. But Brother Yanis, who was a seaman before he became a monk, thought they came from the mainland to the north and he knew their language a little. He has the courage of a lion. While we hid, he confronted them and told them they could see for themselves that we had no gold, nor fine clothes, nor women.

"If you kill us," said Yanis, "or desecrate our church, you are in danger of eternal damnation, but if you spare us, we shall pray for you, that all men shall be brothers, as Jesus commanded." They had a long discussion and then departed down the mountainside back to their ship, grumbling and carrying-off our largest jar of olive oil as booty. Every day we pray for them. They have never returned.

One of them left his dagger outside the church, by mistake, and it has jewels in the handle so perhaps he captured it from a king. Brother Costas has become quite attached to this beautiful dagger and uses it for dividing the bread dough and for skinning goats.

Although we all share the cooking, Costas is the best cook so it seems right that he should have first use of the dagger. He also has a vivid imagination. None of us here can read but we know the Gospel stories from our years of training at the mother house, and we often discuss the lifestyle of the early disciples because we try to model our life on theirs as much as possible. One evening we were discussing what might have happened to Mary, the mother of Jesus, in later life. To the best of our knowledge there is no mention of her in the Bible after Jesus went to heaven.

The next morning Costas told us he had had a dream that Mary had found it very difficult to accept that the disciples would have the strength to pass on the good news of the Gospel, after Jesus had gone to heaven. They did tell the good news, of course, otherwise we would not be here now in this place, but, in Costas' dream, Mary became inconsolable and killed herself with a dagger.

"Costas, you are obsessed with that dagger," said Yanis, and Costas replied, "No, I am not obsessed. I do believe that is what happened and the message for us is not to lose heart."

We debated this for days and when Father Abbot sent Brother Nikos, the finest artist in our monastery, to spend the summer with us and paint frescoes in our little church, Costas asked him to include a picture of Mary's death. Nikos said he had never painted such a scene and did not know if it was right to do so, with such thin evidence of its truth, and without the express permission of Father Abbot. We spent much time talking about this matter and had not come to any conclusion when summer was ending and the wind was very strong, making it dangerous to walk the cliff path to the big monastery. Only a year ago, Brother Tomas had been blown off this path and fell to his death down the huge cliff face. We were not even able to recover his body.

So we decided to ask Brother Adonis in his hermit's cell, because he is close to God. The next day when Costas was putting his food on the window ledge of the cell, he told Adonis about our discussion and asked his opinion. Adonis did not answer a word and sometimes we think he may have been struck dumb, but more likely he has just got out of the habit of talking. Costas said, "Brother Adonis, God be with you. I hope you have heard my question and I do understand that you do not have an answer at present. Please will you meditate upon it. I am putting the dagger on your food ledge, pointing north. If you think it right that Brother Nikos should paint Mary the mother of Jesus with the dagger, please point the dagger to the east, towards Jerusalem where these events took place. If you think it is not right, point it west, towards Rome."

For two whole weeks the dagger remained untouched, pointing north, and Costas was quite bad tempered because he had to revert to his blunt old knife to skin our weekly goat. We knew that Adonis was alive because he took the food regularly from the ledge, even though we could not see him behind his wall, and he never spoke. "What if he points it south," grumbled Costas, "what shall we do then?" Then one day when we took his food, we heard Adonis singing a psalm and the dagger was pointing east to Jerusalem, with a stone each side of the point to indicate that it had not been turned by the wind. Nikos happily accepted this sign and painted the picture beautifully; it is just below one of his regular pictures of Abraham and Isaac.

All this happened some years ago and we are told that Brother Nikos has never painted this scene again, so our wall picture is very rare. May God preserve it. Perhaps one day, in His good time, visitors will come to Hrisostomas, see the picture and meditate on the meaning of it. But for us, there is much work to be done if we are to survive the coming winter. The barley harvest was good and the olives are nearly ready for picking, so we must find a strong piece of wood to repair the olive press.

We are not downhearted. We praise God and know that we are in His presence in this beautiful place.

10. Letter from a Barbary Pirate

In 1628 Henry Smith, a wealthy London merchant, set aside £1000 for the relief of Christians who had been enslaved by Barbary pirates operating off the coast of what is now Turkey. In the 18th century there were ferocious raids on Amorgos and pirates 'controlled the harbours'. In 2016 the Henry Smith Charity (Registered Charity 230102) has an income of £12.8 million and still includes among its objects, 'the relief of those persons who have been slaves or serfs who are in need or distress... or for preventing their seizure.' Maybe from time to time the Trustees will have received letters such as the following.

Dear Trustees, October 1795

I write as a bona fide Barbary pirate to make application for a grant for a young lady named Sultana whom we captured and enslaved some years ago. We have, of course, taught her the necessities of life aboard our pirate ship, *Black Swan*. She can reef the mainsail in a gale, tie a bowline on the bight and swim with a cutlass clenched between her teeth.

However, due the transient nature of a pirate's life, we consider she needs some finishing touches to her education. Perhaps some history about piracy on our coasts would be useful, and some teaching about the theological justification of God-fearing pirates? We think some training in sword play would stand her in good stead and she needs instruction in sewing black eye patches for our murderous crew. Alternatively you may wish to offer a ransom to free this young lady from our clutches.

You may wish to check my piratical credentials before making a decision. I am proud to tell you that we have ransacked at least twenty villages on the islands off our coast during the last few years. Rape and pillage have been effectively employed. Prisoners taken have been very few but we have thought it expedient to carry off a number of voluptuous Greek young women, like Sultana. Our mate,

Black Pete, will corroborate these facts (and if he doesn't I'll cut his liver out. Ho ho ho).

I am willing to voyage to Londinium for interview at your command. I hear there is anchorage on the river near your Tower and rich pickings for us in the nearby Citadel where your corrupt money lenders and bankers crouch over heaps of ducats and gold moidores, stolen from the Portugeese.

Our visit may need to be brief because the customs men and school attendance officers are harrying us, not to mention your redcoats and their muskets. Neither have your Social Services been much help to us and keep mentioning a 'means test' with regard to all the bounty in our hold. I hope you Trustees will agree to make a grant for the benefit of Sultana and suggest that 100 gold bars will render you protection from our ships.

In the event of you refusing to make such a grant, we will blow you to smithereens.

Yours sincerely,

(signed in blood)   Long John Hassan (Barbary Pirate)

11. What to do about the devil

The three of them were walking in remote country on an island in the Aegean sea. Their names are irrelevant but I will call them Peter, James and John, for each was concerned for the coming of the Kingdom, like Jesus' first disciples in the Gospel narratives.

'It's the devil of a hot day', said Peter.
'Talking of devils,' said James, 'what's yours?'

'My devil,' said Peter, 'my burden is loneliness. I find it difficult to make lasting relationships. I am diminished.'

'My devil is anxiety,' said James, 'I am anxious and troubled by matters which I know are of little consequence. What shall we have for supper? Is my dentist appointment to-morrow or next week?'

'My devil is money,' said John, 'I am not rich as the world measures riches, I have no large house or car or motor yacht, but I have more money than most people. It is a burden, I don't know what to do with it.'

The three agree that these devils prevent them from living life to the full. They walk on in silence, contemplating, and then in the heat of the day they come to a small whitewashed church, cool, quiet, and miles from the nearest habitation. The island has many such churches and this one is dedicated to St George; there are ikons of him, a blond young man on a splendid horse. But a devil in the guise of a dragon with fearsome fangs and a hideous scaly body has its tail wound round the horse's hind leg, thus preventing George from riding out into the world. However, George has a lance which he is thrusting down the throat of the devilish dragon, forcing it to release its grip on his horse and enabling him to pursue his destiny, free of devils.

Peter, James and John stay silent in the church, each considering how he might overcome his personal devilish dragon of loneliness, anxiety, surplus. Then they share the bread they have brought and, in the sharing, they are not lonely or anxious and there is enough bread, not too much or too little, no surplus.

And they pray for the world and for each other.

A Guide for Swimmers

Many miles of the coast of *Amorgos* are huge cliffs with no access to the sea but the island also has numerous beaches and coves accessible for swimming in the wonderful clear blue Aegean water. Even in summer, only a few beaches are ever crowded (*Ormos, Mouros, Aghia Anna*) and some are seldom visited at all either by locals or visitors.

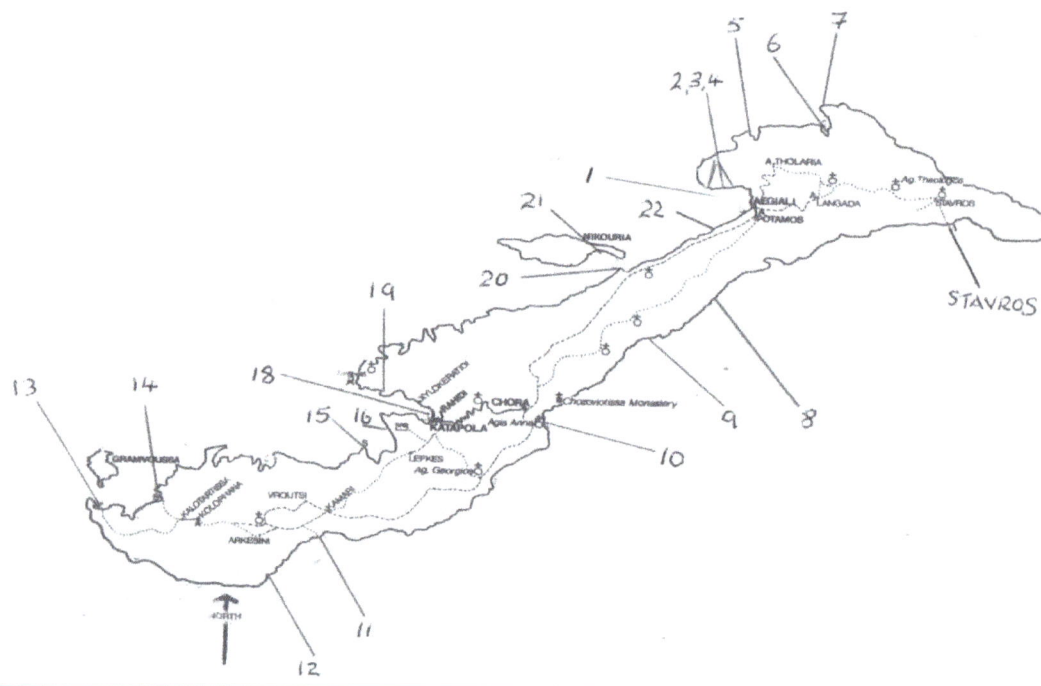

Ten beaches are accessible by road (swimwear required, otherwise not) and a further eight are near paths. Three others (6,7,9) can only be reached by crossing rough country without paths and one (21) by swimming or by boat. There are a few remote coves still to be discovered. Some can only be reached by sea.

Due to the prevailing wind some of the north-facing beaches are spoilt by rubbish and plastic (16) but the south-facing ones are cleaner with wonderfully clear deep water. In the 1990's there was oil on some beaches, caused by ships cleaning their tanks at sea, but this now seems under control and it is rare to find any remaining.

There are several good distance swims:

Ormos (1) beach to the ferry quay. 200 metres (eight lengths of a 25 metre pool) each way. Beware of fishing boats and ferries, which are not expecting to encounter swimmers away from the beach.

Aghios Pavlos (20) to *Nikouria* island (21). 300 metres each way. Beware of currents at certain states of the tide. Very sharp rocks make it difficult to get ashore on the island.

Ormos(1) to *Psiliamos* (3) 900 metres. Companion needed to carry your clothes unless you swim both ways which would take about an hour.

Distances and spellings are taken from the 1:35,000 *Amorgos* map published by Anavasi, Athens, www.mountains.gr. GPS is useful but not always satisfactory in this precipitous country and walkers are recommended to use a map.

R= Access by road. P= Access by path. N= No easy access.

1. R   *Ormos (Egiali)*. 1 km sand. Excellent swimming.

2. R   *Levrosos* (aka second bay). Good sand.

3. P   *Psiliamos* (aka third bay). Mostly stony but some sand. Tamarisk trees provide shade.

4. P   *Chocklakas* (aka fourth bay). Five minutes cliff walk beyond *Psiliamos*. Mostly stony. Good shade under trees at the west end of the bay.

5. P   *Mikri Vlichadha*. Path from the village of *Tholaria* steep but in good condition. Good swimming. Beware of plastic.

6. N   *Meghali Vlichadha*. Good swimming but access is by a 150 metre scramble down a near vertical cliff-face (see story "And Who is my Neighbour"). There is an alternative access route on the east side of the bay but considerable care is needed for either of these routes and neither should be attempted by anyone except experienced walkers/climbers. Take a mobile phone and tell home base where you are going.

7. N   *Limenari*. A stream (dry in summer) runs into the sea at the northern tip of the island. There is no path and the rocks are sharp making access to the water rather hazardous. From here going southeast along the coast there are massive cliffs and no access to the sea for 13 km until *Stavros* is reached. Here there is an old jetty for the long-disused bauxite mine south of *Stavros* church. The path from the church to the mine is steep and in poor condition. Not recommended.

8. P   *Halara*. No beach but a lovely small natural harbour and very deep clear water. Beware of sea urchins.

9. N   *Masticha* bay. Smooth rock slabs provide good access to deep water. There is no path but a rough descent from *Hrisostomos* church takes about 30 minutes. A Cycladic figure (*kouros*) was found near here in the 19th century and is now in the National Archaeological Museum in Athens.

10. R   *Aghia Anna*. Small sand beach below the *Chozoviatissa* monastery. Popular for visitors based in *Chora*. Also a stony beach.

11 R *Mouros*. Approached by a road from *Kamari*. Sand and rock slabs. Good swimming.

12 P *Amoudi*. Small, stony, remote. Marked path from *Arkesini*.

13 R *Kalotaritissa*. Sheltered anchorage at the west end of the island. Sand but shallow. Popular for those who like to go to the end of the road. Sometimes a local boat owner will ferry visitors across to the deserted island of *Gramvousa*

14 R *Paradhisa* (paradise !). Small sand bay. Good swimming in deep water.

15 R *Kato Kambos*. Sheltered anchorage. Approached by a rough road from *Kolofana*. Interesting historic church. Bay is shallow with a stony bottom. Poor swimming.

16 P *Aghia Sarada*. Good sand bay and often a gentle swell from the north. There is a surprising sand bar in the bay. The foreshore is littered.

17 P *Finikies*. A rather dull beach at the end of a track. Hardly worth a visit.

18 R *Katapola*. A narrow unexciting town beach.

19 P *Panteleimon*. South facing. Better for swimming than *Katapola* port. As an alternative to walking there is a regular small ferry boat from the port.

20 R *Aghios Pavlos*. A tongue of land runs out from the shore and looks inviting but it is unredeemably stony. Take-off point to swim to *Nikouria*.

21 N *Nikouria* has lovely sand beaches but they are a kilometre from the rocky shore where swimmers are likely to land. Wear beach shoes or suffer cuts to feet and legs from spiky rocks.

22 R 'Swell bay'. Small hidden roadside bay about one kilometre west of *Egiali*. It is unsheltered and open to the swell from the open sea to the north. Exhilarating deep water swimming, but be careful of heavy surf on windy days

www.ingramcontent.com/pod-product-compliance
Lightning Source LLC
Chambersburg PA
CBHW042122100526
44587CB00025B/4154